FICIAL
ELSEA FC
ANNUAL 2016

Antill, Richard Godden, James Sugrue

ey Scott-Peterson

tion

range Communications Ltd., Edinburgh, under licence from
ing Limited. www.chelseafc.com. Printed in the EU.

ade to ensure the accuracy of information within this
lishers cannot be held responsible for any errors or omissions.
ose of the author and do not necessarily represent those of the
ll club. All rights reserved.

FC; Press Association; Action Images and Shutterstock.

-8

CONTENTS

Welcome, Chelsea fans, to the official annual of the Premier League champions! After an incredible 2014/15 season, in which José Mourinho led the Blues to success in the Premier League and Capital One Cup, our defence of the title is now well under way. We hope you are enjoying the new season and getting behind the team. Now you can feed your Chelsea obsession after the final whistle blows because these pages are full of facts, stats, pics and games that will keep even the most ardent Blues fan on their toes. Relive our triumphant season, check out the record-breaking stats and find out what makes our players tick – it's all in these next 56 pages of pure Chelsea bliss, so get stuck in!

And remember...
Keep the blue flag flying high!

Stamford and Bridget!

STORY OF THE SEASON

The Blues enjoyed a stunning 2014/15 season, lifting the Premier League and Capital One Cup. In case you've forgotten, here's how they did it...

THE 2014/15 CAMPAIGN kicked off at newly promoted Burnley, who gave us a bit of a scare by taking the lead. But Chelsea responded with an early contender for Goal of the Season when André Schürrle finished off a brilliant team move. Diego Costa and Branislav Ivanovic also scored to make sure we got off to a winning start.

IT WAS RAINING GOALS at Goodison Park when the Blues came to town at the end of August – at one point we were treated to five in 10 second-half minutes! Diego Costa scored in the first minute and the last to continue his great start to the season, and we took the outright lead of the Barclays Premier League table. It is where we would remain for the rest of the season...

DIEGO'S HAT-TRICK came in the 4-2 win against Swansea. In the previous season our strikers scored 19 Premier League goals between them, but Diego already had seven in four games! With Cesc Fàbregas pulling the strings in midfield and bringing up his sixth assist of the campaign, things were looking good.

THE FIRST HEAVYWEIGHT

clash of the season at Stamford Bridge, and a knockout blow delivered by the team in the blue corner! Arsenal didn't know what hit them when Eden Hazard jinked through their defence – all they could do was foul him! But that's no good when the Belgian is so cool from the penalty spot. When Diego Costa scored a brilliant lob in the second half, it was time for the Gunners to throw in the towel.

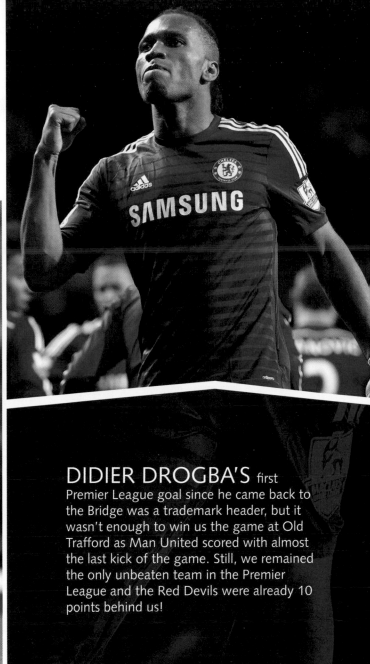

DIDIER DROGBA'S first Premier League goal since he came back to the Bridge was a trademark header, but it wasn't enough to win us the game at Old Trafford as Man United scored with almost the last kick of the game. Still, we remained the only unbeaten team in the Premier League and the Red Devils were already 10 points behind us!

Simon Mignolet thought he'd kept out **GARY CAHILL'S SHOT,** but the Goal Decision System doesn't lie! It was a crucial effort for the Blues as it brought us level against Liverpool at Anfield before Diego Costa scored again to give us a second straight win at the home of the Reds just a few months after we had ruined their title challenge!

IT WAS TOO EASY for Chelsea when Spurs visited the Bridge, especially when Loic Remy brushed Jan Vertonghen aside on his way to scoring our third goal of the game! After this win it meant Spurs hadn't won at the Bridge in 23 Premier League visits!

JOSÉ MOURINHO and plenty of football pundits agreed that our win against Stoke before Christmas was the perfect away performance. No wonder Cesc was so happy when he scored the goal that helped clinch the three points! Top at Christmas and loving it...

IT TOOK OSCAR 50 SECONDS to give us the lead at Swansea, and it was 4-0 by half-time after he netted another and Diego Costa scored two. By the end we had racked up five, and Gary Cahill said it was the best we had played as a team in the whole season – and that's saying something, as the boys weren't short on great team performances!

NO DIEGO COSTA? No problem for Loic Remy! The French striker scored against Manchester City at the Bridge, but the game finished 1-1, just as it did at the Etihad Stadium earlier in the season.

JOSÉ RECKONS he's never won a league title without his side nicking the odd win late on, and Everton was one of the few times we left it until the last minute. Willian's face tells you all you need to know about how important his goal was.

JT PICKED A GREAT MOMENT to score his first cup final goal for the Blues! Spurs were no match for the skipper or his team-mates at Wembley Stadium as we recorded a 2-0 win to secure the trophy for the fifth time in our history.

11

COMING FROM TWO GOALS BEHIND, the boys had to show all of their fighting spirit to beat Hull City 3-2 at the KC Stadium. Eden Hazard scored a beauty, but it was Loic Remy's late goal which gave us the win which moved us a step closer to the title.

WHO'S THE MAN
behind the mask? Cesc Fàbregas, of course! The Spaniard wore it to keep his broken nose protected and it certainly didn't hinder him on the pitch as he scored a brilliant late winner against QPR.

NOW YOU SEE IT, NOW YOU DON'T! David de Gea may have been picked in the PFA
Team of the Season, but that didn't stop Eden Hazard sticking the ball through his legs to score the only goal of the game v Man United. The result allowed the Blues to put one hand on the Premier League trophy...

AND THAT DREAM BECAME A REALITY a fortnight later when the Blues beat
Crystal Palace to be confirmed as Premier League champions. It was only the first week of May and there were still three matches to be played.

THE BOYS HAD TO WAIT a long time to finally get the chance to lift the trophy, but it was
worth the wait! A 3-1 win over Sunderland was the perfect way to get the fans in the party mood, although JT, Petr Cech and Didier Drogba were more than used to that as they lifted the trophy for the fourth time. Only Man United have won it more times than that!

13

RECORD BREAKERS

AS WELL AS WINNING TWO TROPHIES LAST SEASON, the Blues also broke a number of records along the way. Here is a selection of the best.

MAJESTIC MOURINHO

José Mourinho guided the Blues to a record number of days at the top of the Premier League table. We spent 274 days in first place, beating Man United's 262 from 1993/94.

The Blues boss also became the quickest Premier League manager to reach 400 points and also the fastest manager to reach 100 Premier League clean sheets. The man in second place for both of those statistics? Former United gaffer Sir Alex Ferguson!

CAPTAIN FANTASTIC

Last season was John Terry's 17th in the Chelsea first team, and definitely one of his best. He played every single minute of every Premier League game – becoming only the second outfield player ever to achieve that. He also became the club's leading appearance-maker of all time in the Premier League, breaking Frank Lampard's record. And that's not all, because JT became the highest-scoring Premier League defender, taking his tally to 39. All that and he got to lift two trophies! He really is our Captain, Leader, Legend!

GOAL MACHINE

Diego Costa got off to a blistering start in his first season as a Blue. He became just the second player ever to score in his first four games for the club and is only the fourth to score 20 Premier League goals in a season. The others are Jimmy Floyd Hasselbaink (twice), Didier Drogba (twice) and Frank Lampard.

109	109	102	91	74
CHELSEA	ARSENAL	MAN UNITED	MAN CITY	LIVERPOOL

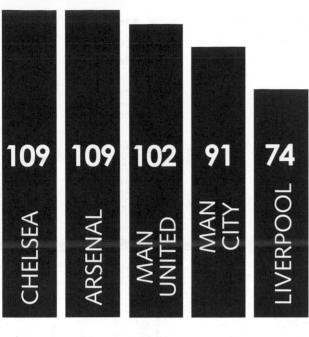

ENTERTAINERS

No side scored more goals in all competitions than Chelsea last season.

WINNING WAYS

The Blues were only beaten four times in all competitions last season, beating our previous club record of six defeats. We were also the only side in all four English divisions not to lose at home in the league. On top of that, no team conceded fewer league goals at home than our nine.

4	10	10	14	18
CHELSEA	ARSENAL	MAN UNITED	MAN CITY	LIVERPOOL

BEST OF THE REST

The 2014/15 campaign was Chelsea's record 26th-straight season in the top flight, beating the previous club record set between 1930 and 1962.

Dominic Solanke became our youngest Champions League debutant when he came on as a substitute at home to Maribor, aged 17 years, 38 days.

We went unbeaten for a club record 21 games at the start of the season, beating the previous record of 16 set in 2005/06.

We had the best away record in the Premier League with 38 points from 19 matches and won more away games (11) than any other team.

We kept the most clean sheets (17) and conceded the fewest league goals (32).

15

INSIDER!

We all know what the Blues get up to on the pitch, but what about when they're not winning football matches? We pick out some of the best behind-the-scenes pictures from the 2014/15 season.

Diego Costa is a bit outnumbered by the Chelsea Academy Under-8s players during a kick-about. The first-team join the youngsters for a game at Cobham training ground every Christmas.

Eden Hazard takes on some Chelsea fans in a special game of EA Sports' FIFA 15 in the pitchside dugout at Stamford Bridge.

José Mourinho takes on the Ice Bucket Challenge at Cobham with help from his assistant first-team coaches Silvino Louro and Rui Faria.

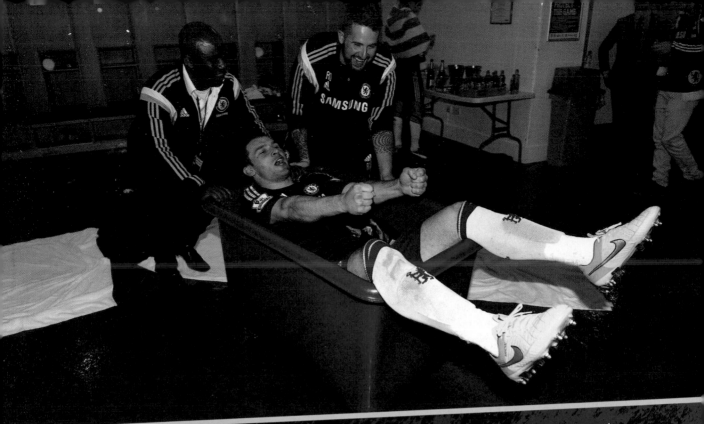

Branislav Ivanovic does his best racing driver impression while celebrating winning the Premier League title in the Stamford Bridge changing room.

Thibaut Courtois, Izzy Brown, Eden Hazard and Kurt Zouma help Stamford the Lion celebrate the Songkran Thai New Year with a traditional water fight at Cobham training ground.

17

EDEN WINS BIG AT AWARDS

There was a huge amount of recognition for Chelsea stars at the end-of-season awards, and deservedly so considering how the Blues performed in the 2014/15 campaign.

Eden Hazard was the big winner, collecting no less than three trophies, and that's not including the club's awards, which you can read about on page 35. Firstly, his fellow footballers voted for him as he won the Professional Footballers' Association (PFA) Players' Player of the Year honour. That means every time you saw the Belgian winger skip around an opponent last season, those players had as much respect for Eden's silky skills as we do.

"I just want to say thank you to the players who voted for me – it is always good to have an individual honour, but the most important thing was winning the league," said the 24-year-old.

"What I did is play very well and Chelsea played very well. I don't know if I deserve to win, but it is good for me. I started the season not to be PFA Player of the Year but it was in my head – I want to be the

best and I hope one day I can win lots of trophies." The country's sports journalists obviously enjoyed watching our wing wizard in action as they gave him the Footballer Writers' Association Player of the Year award. Hazard became only the third Chelsea player to win that honour, following Gianfranco Zola in 1997 and Frank Lampard in 2005. And let's hope the Hazard trophy cabinet is a big one because Eden was also named the Barclays Premier League Player of the Season.

Having guided the Blues to two trophies last season, José Mourinho deservedly picked up the Barclays Manager of the Season honour, making it a hat-trick for the Special One after he won the same trophy twice during his first spell in charge of the club, in 2005 and 2006. That means the only manager to have won the award more times is arguably the greatest of all time, Sir Alex Ferguson.

EDEN HAZARD with his PFA Players' Player of the Year award

The ultimate six-aside team

Hazard wasn't the only Blues player to be recognised at the PFA awards, as five of his team-mates were named alongside him in the PFA Premier League Team of the Year. With Chelsea conceding the fewest amount of goals in the Premier League, three of our defenders – John Terry, Gary Cahill and Branislav Ivanovic made it in the team. There was also a place for Nemanja Matic and Diego Costa after they both had excellent seasons.

Chelsea Ladies star Ji So-Yun was another Blue to go home from the awards ceremony with a trophy after she was voted PFA Women's Players' Player of the Year, just beating her team-mate Eniola Aluko who came second. The duo are two of the best attacking talents in the FA Women's Super League, and both were named in the Team of the Year.

JI SO-YUN celebrates her win with host Jake Humphrey and Chelsea Ladies manager Emma Hayes

DID YOU KNOW?

Eden Hazard is only the second Chelsea star to win the main PFA award, after John Terry collected the trophy in 2005. Hazard did take home the PFA's Young Player honour last year. What next for the brilliant Belgian?

Hazard wasn't able to make it to the Football Writers' awards ceremony because he had just had three wisdom teeth removed – ouch! José Mourinho won the Barclays Manager of the Season award, but he was not voted Manager of the Month once in 2014/15. Good job they saw sense in the end!

Images courtesy of PA Images.

ASMIR BEGOVIC

Born: Trebinje, Yugoslavia, 20.6.87
Height: 1.98m
Signed from: Stoke City (July 2015)

Did You Know?

Asmir scored the second longest goal ever in a competitive football match when he netted from 91.9m for Stoke City against Southampton's Artur Boruc in November 2013!

JAMAL BLACKMAN

Born: Croydon, England, 27.10.93
Height: 1.99m
Turned pro: July 2011

Did You Know?

Jamal's professional debut came during a loan spell at Middlesbrough against Liverpool, which ended with the joint highest-scoring penalty shoot-out in English professional football!

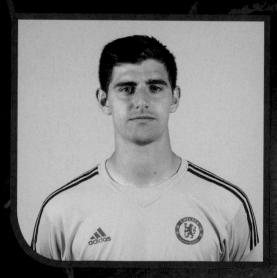

THIBAUT COURTOIS

Born: Bree, Belgium, 11.5.92
Height: 1.99m
Signed from: Genk (July 2011)
Appearances: 39
Clean sheets: 16

Did You Know?

"Thibauting" became a craze in Belgium throughout 2013, which involved fans emulating a classic Courtois save in a random location!

DEFENDERS

CESAR AZPILICUETA

Born: Pamplona, Spain, 28.8.89
Height: 1.78m
Signed from: Marseille (August 2012)
Appearances: 132
Goals: 1

Did You Know?

During the off-season, Cesar spends time back in Zizur Mayor, where he lived with his parents, to coach local kids between the age of six and 14.

GARY CAHILL

Born: Sheffield, England, 19.12.85
Height: 1.93m
Signed from: Bolton Wanderers (January 2012)
Appearances: 157
Goals: 13

Did You Know?

Gary has spent three full seasons as a Chelsea - and two of them have ended with him being named in the PFA Premier League Team of the Year!

PAPY DJILOBODJI

Born: Kaolack, Senegal, 01.12.88
Height: 1.92m
Signed from: Nantes (September 2015)

Did You Know?

Papy has been a team-mate of former Chelsea striker Demba Ba in the Senegalese national team since making his debut in 2013.

DEFENDERS

BRANISLAV IVANOVIC

Born: Sremska Mitrovica, Serbia, 22.2.84
Height: 1.85m
Signed from: Lokomotiv Moscow (January 2008)
Appearances: 318
Goals: 31

Did You Know?

Branner was named as Chelsea's vice-captain for the 2015/16 season, seven years after he signed for the club.

BABA RAHMAN

Born: Tamale, Ghana, 02.07.94
Height: 1.79m
Signed from: Augsburg (August 2015)

Did You Know?

Rahman made more successful tackles than any other player in the German Bundesliga in the 2014/15 season.

JOHN TERRY

Born: Barking, England, 7.12.80
Height: 1.87m
Turned pro: March 1998
Appearances: 670
Goals: 65

Did You Know?

JT is the highest-scoring defender in Premier League history - a fact which is even more impressive when you consider none of his goals have come from penalties or set-pieces!

KURT ZOUMA

Born: Lyon, France, 27.10.94
Height: 1.90m
Signed from: Saint-Etienne (January 2014)
Appearances: 26
Goals: 2

Did You Know?

Although he is mainly a centre-back, Kurt played as a defensive-midfielder in the 2015 Capital One Cup final - and he looked like he had played there his entire life!

MIDFIELDERS

CESC FABREGAS
Born: Arenys de Mar, Spain, 4.5.87
Height: 1.75m
Signed from: Barcelona (June 2014)
Appearances: 47
Goals: 5

Did You Know?
In his debut season as a Blue, Cesc recorded a fab assists tally of 18 in the Premier League, which was seven more than his nearest challenger.

EDEN HAZARD
Born: La Louvière, Belgium, 7.1.91
Height: 1.73m
Signed from: Lille (July 2012)
Appearances: 163
Goals: 49

Did You Know?
In the 2014/15 season, Eden made his 400th appearance as a professional footballer. He was only 24 years old at the time!

RUBEN LOFTUS-CHEEK
Born: Lewisham, England, 23.1.96
Height: 1.91m
Turned pro: January 2013
Appearances: 4
Goals: 0

Did You Know?
When he made his first Chelsea start against Liverpool, Ruben completed every single one of his passes during the 60 minutes he spent on the pitch!

NEMANJA MATIC
Born: Vrelo-Ub, Serbia, 1.8.88
Height: 1.94m
Signed from: Benfica (January 2014)
Appearances: 71
Goals: 3

Did You Know?
Nemanja scored his first international goal for Serbia against Portugal with an incredible overhead kick!

JOHN MIKEL OBI
Born: Jos, Nigeria, 22.4.87
Height: 1.88m
Signed from: Lyn Oslo (June 2006)
Appearances: 339
Goals: 5

Did You Know?
John Terry is the only player at Chelsea who has been in the first-team squad longer than Mikel!

OSCAR
Born: Americana, Brazil, 9.9.91
Height: 1.79m
Signed from: Internacional (July 2012)
Appearances: 151
Goals: 30

Did You Know?
Oscar won Chelsea's Goal of the Season award for the second time in 2015, having previously won it in 2013 after scoring a worldie in his first Champions League game for the club!

MIDFIELDERS

PEDRO

Born: Santa Cruz de Tenerife, Spain, 28.7.87
Height: 1.70m
Signed from: Barcelona (August 2015)

Did You Know?

Pedro became the 87th Chelsea player to score on their debut for the club when he netted against West Bromwich Albion in August 2015.

RAMIRES

Born: Barra do Pirai, Brazil, 24.3.87
Height: 1.80m
Signed from: Benfica (August 2010)
Appearances: 224
Goals: 30

Did You Know?

In his five years with Chelsea, Rami has won the Premier League, FA Cup, Capital One Cup, Champions League and Europa League. That's more than most clubs have won in their entire history!

BERTRAND TRAORE

Born: Bobo-Dioulasso, Burkina Faso, 06.09.95
Height: 1.81m
Signed from: Bobo-Dioulasso (January 2014)

Did You Know?

Bertrand scored 17 times in the Dutch Eredivisie in the 2014/15 season to help Vitesse Arnhem qualify for the Europa League.

WILLIAN

Born: Ribeirão Pires, Brazil, 9.8.88
Height: 1.75m
Appearances: 91
Goals: 8
Signed from: Anzhi Makhachkala (August 2013)

Did You Know?

After leaving Brazil, Willian played football in Ukraine and Russia before moving to England. Clearly he prefers the cold weather to the sunshine of his homeland!

FORWARDS

DIEGO COSTA
Born: Lagarto, Brazil, 7.10.88
Height: 1.88m
Signed from: Atletico Madrid (July 2014)
Appearances: 37
Goals: 21

Did You Know?
Only one player has ever scored 10 top-flight goals for Chelsea in less time than Diego Costa. That man was Jack Cock, who did it in 1919 – almost 100 years ago!

RADAMEL FALCAO
Born: Santa Marta, Colombia, 10.2.86
Height: 1.78m
Signed from: Monaco (July 2015 on loan)

Did You Know?
No one has scored more goals for Colombia than Radamel, who brought up a national record when he netted his 25th goal for his country in June 2015.

KENEDY
Born: Santa Rita do Sapucai, Brazil, 08.2.96
Height: 1.81m
Signed from: Fluminense (August 2015)

Did You Know?
Kenedy's former club Fluminense play their games at the Maracana Stadium in Rio, which is where the 2014 World Cup final was held.

LOIC REMY
Born: Rillieux-la-Pape, France, 2.1.87
Height: 1.85m
Signed from: Queens Park Rangers (August 2014)
Appearances: 29
Goals: 9

Did You Know?
Loic scored a Premier League goal every 99 minutes, on average, during his first season at the Bridge.

WORDSEARCH

Find the words in the grid. Words can go horizontally, vertically and diagonally in all eight directions.

```
T M A M A H O K O Y K T K M
Y F C B S A G E R B A F D T
M V H N R N A I L L I W V P
E E A N O I T A D N U O F R
D R M T J P D Y D A L U K O
A O P D K D H G G L L K H T
C T I M R S C O E V Y Y T S
A S O B C O H R M T Y D S O
L A N L B N F E D T P A Z L
G G S H I T Z M D R D P W A
F E A R E W L N A I A G Q N
J M U R F Y M M D T Z Z L K
L O R C Y V N A M C S T A E
M Y N D F B M U S E U M B H
```

ACADEMY
ADIDAS
ALUKO
BRIDGET
CHAMPIONS
COBHAM

FABREGAS
FOUNDATION
HAZARD
MEGASTORE
MOURINHO
MUSEUM

SHED
SOLANKE
STAMFORD
TERRY
WILLIAN
YOKOHAMA

ON THE SPOT

Pat Nevin and Gigi Salmon, two of the stars of Chelsea TV, sat down with us to give their answers to some of the hottest topics...

WHO IS YOUR FAVOURITE PLAYER IN THE CHELSEA SQUAD?

Pat says:

"It changes all the time. Branislav Ivanovic is always a fave with my family; Diego Costa makes me laugh most, and I probably most admire John Terry as a player. But it has to be Eden Hazard. We played in very similar positions and had some similarities in style, but it's mostly because I love watching skill and being entertained."

Gigi says:

"I could run through most of the squad because they are a pleasure to watch and it has been great getting to know them, but it has to be John Terry. I have known JT for 15 years and watched him grow into the player he is today. He is a fantastic leader whose blood runs blue.

WHAT HAS BEEN YOUR FAVOURITE INTERVIEW?

Pat says:

"I found José Mourinho to be intriguing, intelligent and very forthcoming. I like people who give answers you don't expect and José certainly does that more than most. I also like learning about new things, and if you ask him sensible questions and listen to the answers there is always plenty to be learned from him."

Gigi says:

"The one who stands out is the late, great Lord Attenborough, who was the club's Life President. He was an amazing man who had so many great stories to tell from movies he had starred in and the Academy Award-winning films he directed. And then there was his lifelong support and passion for Chelsea, which stood head and shoulders above everything else."

WHAT MAKES CHELSEA TV THE BEST CHANNEL IN THE WORLD?

Pat says:
"It is informative and interesting about the history of the club. On top of that, everyone behind the scenes at the channel, which is based inside Stamford Bridge, are lovely people to work with. I do not think I have ever worked with such a dedicated, yet constantly nice bunch of folk in my entire life!"

Gigi says:
"We are lucky enough to be invited along with the players wherever they go to be able to give you amazing behind-the-scenes access, from the Academy right through to the first team. From the moment you wake up and switch on to the moment you go to sleep, you can be surrounded by the Blues. Who could ask for better than that?!"

ROMAN ABRAMOVICH GIVES YOU A BLANK CHEQUE – WHO DO YOU SIGN FOR CHELSEA?

Pat says:
"I thought about this long and hard – okay, three seconds – and decided on Lionel Messi. As I said about Eden Hazard, I love being entertained and Messi is among the best in the business when it comes to that…"

Gigi says:
"While no team in the world would turn down Messi, what if a blank cheque allowed us to make our own player? We could try mixing together the best bits of Messi with a touch of Cristiano Ronaldo to see what we got. Then, if it allowed us to bring a player back, then I could add in a bit of Zinedine Zidane, who had a fiery streak but was great to watch."

ON THE SPOT

WHAT HAS BEEN YOUR BEST MOMENT FOLLOWING CHELSEA?

Pat says:
"Playing for the club was even more enjoyable than watching and following, to be honest. Having said that, there have been many highlights to watch. Maybe it has to be the Champions League victory, which is right alongside the first Premier League title win."

Gigi says:
"It is really hard to narrow it down to just one, but it's got to be 19 May 2012 when Chelsea won the Champions League. The build-up on Chelsea TV was amazing, the night itself incredible and I had the pleasure of working alongside a host of former Blues. The parade the following day was mind-blowing, although it does hurt when you get hit by big lumps of celery!"

IF YOU COULD INTERVIEW ANY FORMER CHELSEA PLAYER, WHO WOULD IT BE AND WHAT WOULD YOU ASK THEM?

Pat says:
"Maybe if I could have another interview with Gianfranco Zola I would ask him more about his early life and how he developed his skills. We have chatted many times and actually played together once (I love this picture), but every time I meet him I think of a dozen more questions I meant to ask him as soon as I've left!"

Gigi says:
"Like Pat, it would be Gianfranco Zola – again. I was lucky enough to fly out to his home in Sardinia a few years ago to interview him and I could have spoken to him for hours but we had a plane home to catch! So I would like to carry on that conversation. He is a true legend of the game and any chance to speak to him again would be great."

JOHN TERRY is not only Chelsea's most successful captain of all-time, he is also the highest scoring defender in the Premier League's history! We take a look at JT's goal-scoring record...

JT: PREMIER LEAGUE'S DEADLIEST DEFENDER

John Terry's goal against Liverpool in the third-from-last game of the 2014/15 Premier League season made him the highest scoring defender since the league began in 1992.

With 39 Premier League goals to his name, Chelsea's most successful captain of all-time has ensured that the record books will also remember him for his deadliness in front of the opposition goal.

LOOK, NO PENALTIES!

Last season, JT struck five times in the league alone (he scored eight in total) and if you need another reason to be impressed by his stats, just take a look at the three players below him on the Premier Leagues goalscoring defenders chart. David Unsworth, Ian Harte and Leighton Baines all took (or take) penalties for their clubs, with Unsworth and Baines scoring more than half of their league goals from the spot.

Terry, meanwhile, has never taken a Premier League penalty and yet he still tops the list.

JOHN TERRY'S GOALS
(stats correct at the end of the 2014/15 season)

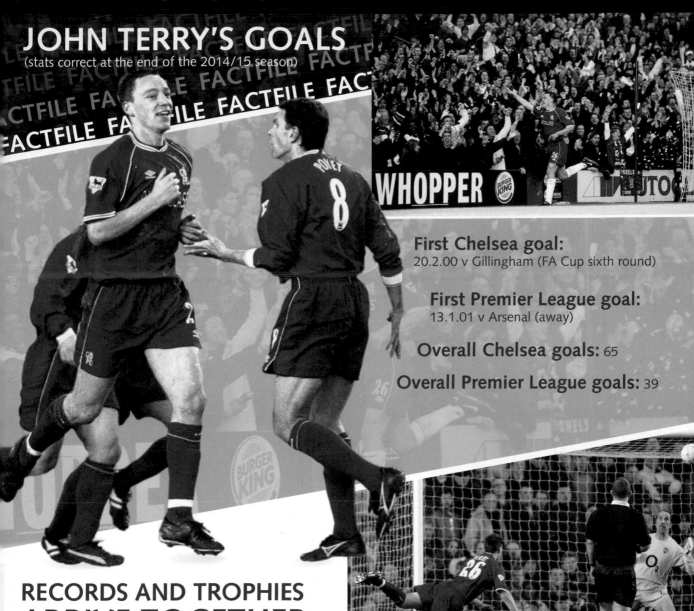

First Chelsea goal:
20.2.00 v Gillingham (FA Cup sixth round)

First Premier League goal:
13.1.01 v Arsenal (away)

Overall Chelsea goals: 65

Overall Premier League goals: 39

RECORDS AND TROPHIES
ARRIVE TOGETHER

Terry broke the scoring record in the game after Chelsea secured the league title against Crystal Palace towards the end of last season. In typical fashion, he explained that the team's achievement always comes before any personal glory, although quietly he was very pleased with his record.

"I'm delighted defensively first and foremost, and it's an added bonus if I can chip in with a fair few goals," Terry said, pointing out that he is a defender first. "I've done that and this goal takes me clear as the highest scoring defender in Premier League history. I'm delighted with that personally, but being champions is the one I really wanted."

DIDYOUKNOW?

JT has scored more goals against Arsenal than any other team, having hit the back of the net five times against the Gunners.

He scored in 15 consecutive Premier League campaigns from 2000/01 through to 2014/15.

His eight goals in all competitions during 2014/15 was Terry's joint-highest scoring season to date, matching his record in 2004/05.

PLAYER OF THE YEAR 2015

Eden Hazard secured his place among some of Chelsea's biggest-ever legends by winning both our Player of the Year and Players' Player of the Year awards in 2014/15. He is only the second player in history to have been voted as the Blues' best by both the fans and his team-mates in the same season. Plus, having also been our Player of the Year in 2014, he became the fifth person to be named Player of the Year in back-to-back campaigns.

"I just want to say thank you to my team-mates because they work for me," said Hazard. "The season was fantastic, not only for me but for the team. We won two trophies and I got a lot of individual awards. I want to share these trophies with everybody, the fans and the players."

The Belgian winger wasn't joking about winning a lot of awards – the Professional Footballers' Association, Barclays Premier League and the Football Writers' Association all selected him as the best in the business in 2014/15, his most successful season yet for Chelsea. As José Mourinho said: "If you love football, you love Eden Hazard."

SUPER STRIKE!

We all know Brazilians like to play beautiful football and those at Chelsea are no exception, as someone from that country won our Goal of the Season award for the fourth time in the last five years. In 2015 it was Oscar holding the trophy, which he also received in 2013. This time it was for an incredible first-time curling shot with the outside of his foot, scored against Queens Park Rangers in a west London derby.

RISING STAR

Kurt Zouma was handed the Young Player of the Year award by Didier Drogba after the Frenchman's brilliant first season at Stamford Bridge. He signed for Chelsea as a centre-back, but has also done well playing in midfield for the Blues, especially against Tottenham when we won the Capital One Cup final at Wembley.

ONE TO WATCH

The first winner of the new Academy Player of the Year award was striker Dominic Solanke. He scored in every round of the FA Youth Cup and UEFA Youth League as Chelsea won both competitions, made his first-team debut for the Blues in a 6-0 win over Maribor in the UEFA Champions League and scored a total of 41 goals for our Academy teams in 2014/15. Not bad for a teenager!

LEADING LADY

The Chelsea Ladies Player of the Year award went to Eniola Aluko, but the striker couldn't accept the trophy in person as she was away with England getting ready for the World Cup. She did record a video message thanking the fans and her team-mates for the award, though, and manager Emma Hayes got up on stage to sing Aluko's praises.

PLAY LIKE HAZARD

Eden Hazard wasn't just Chelsea's Player of the Year last season, he was voted the best player in England by his fellow professionals and the football writers. He tells us what it takes to play like Hazard...

Take pleasure in playing the game. I think where I am today is almost completely down to my brothers. We were always practising in our back garden, whether it was sunny, raining or snowing. As soon as school finished we would be out there in the back garden playing football. Anyone who is decent at football owes it to the time they spent playing with their family or their friends and in my case it was my brothers. That is when you learn the game.

I always want to do better than my last performance. I want to beat my last performance. Even if you score two goals in a game, the next game you can try to score three. Even at the age of four or five, I always wanted to improve, to better myself. I would see things on TV and I would try to copy them or even improve on them. I was always juggling the ball, trying to beat my record from the day before - I must have spent 300 hours playing and practising tricks.

Never lose confidence in your ability.

You might be having your best four or five minutes of the game, where everything is coming off for you, where you have just tried two or three difficult passes and made them, or you have beaten one or two players with a run, so your confidence is really high and, because of that, you might be more likely to try something than you would 60 or 70 minutes into a terrible game, where nothing was working for

Even in those games where things haven't been working, you still have to try those movements, try to make a difference because attacking players are there for that. In the same way midfielders are there to play good passes and goalkeepers are there to prevent goals, we have to try things.

I know what I am capable of and I know that, in one movement, I can get past someone and create a chance, or score myself. It is about knowing what your capabilities are and being able to do those things.

Most importantly, I need to work for the team. I understand that football is not just played with the ball. The manager and other players have helped me a lot with that. I know my objective is to score, but I also need to help the team when we don't have the ball. I want to win first of all. Even if I score three goals and we lose the game, it's no good for me.

PROGRESS: FIRST-TEAM CHANCES FOR YOUNG BLUES

The 2014/15 season was a good one for young players looking to make their mark. Over the course of the campaign, there were debuts for Dominic Solanke, Andreas Christensen, Ruben Loftus-Cheek and Izzy Brown and further first-team appearances for Nathan Ake.

José Mourinho also included several other Academy graduates in his matchday squads during the campaign. Lewis Baker, Mitchell Beeney, Jamal Blackman and Jeremie Boga were all named as substitutes for the first team last season.

If you have ever wondered what it would feel like to pull on the Chelsea shirt and run out at Stamford Bridge, Loftus-Cheek (pictured preparing to make his debut) put it best of all when he explained how it felt to make his senior debut in a Champions League game against Sporting Lisbon.

"After training on Tuesday, I got a call saying I was in the squad and just that, just being involved, I was really happy with," he said. "It was the best feeling, just to be involved on the bench.

"When we got to the stadium and the game began, it was great – just warming up in front of 30,000 or 40,000 people was crazy, but when I came on it was amazing. Playing in front of that many people is wicked, but when you start playing, that all kind of goes away and you are only focused on the game."

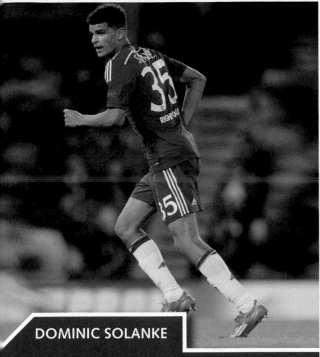

DOMINIC SOLANKE

Date of birth: 14.9.97
Place of birth: Reading
Position: Forward
First-team debut: 21.10.14 v Maribor
(Champions League group stage)

Date of birth: 10.4.96
Place of birth: Allerød, Denmark
Position: Defender
First-team debut: 28.10.14 v Shrewsbury
(Capital One Cup fourth round)

ANDREAS CHRISTENSEN

RUBEN LOFTUS-CHEEK

Date of birth: 23.1.96
Place of birth: Lewisham
Position: Midfielder
First-team debut: 10.12.14 v Sporting
Lisbon (Champions League group stage)

Date of birth: 07.1.97
Place of birth: Peterborough
Position: Forward
First-team debut: 18.5.15 v West Brom
(Premier League)

IZZY BROWN

EUROPEAN SUCCESS: UEFA YOUTH LEAGUE

Many of the youngsters who made their first-team debuts last season were also central to the success of our youth teams, both at home and abroad, in 2014/15. For the first time, Chelsea won the UEFA Youth League, which is an Under-19s version of the Champions League.

The semi-finals and the final were played over a single weekend in Nyon, Switzerland, where UEFA headquarters are based, giving the latter stages a real tournament feel.

Chelsea, coached by Adi Viveash, were the stars of the show, hammering Italian team AS Roma 4-0 in the semi-finals and then beating Ukrainian champions Shakhtar Donetsk 3-2 in the final thanks to two goals from Izzy Brown and one from Dominic Solanke.

It was a big day for all involved, and coach Viveash even got a bit emotional watching his team celebrate.

"It was a really special moment when Izzy lifted the trophy," he said. "We went up the steps and it felt very real – you couldn't help but start to get emotional with the paper coming down, the music playing and Michel Platini giving out medals. That doesn't happen every day. To win the tournament and become Under-19s European champions is a marvellous achievement."

DOMINANCE: ANOTHER FA YOUTH CUP TRIUMPH

Last season, our Under-18s won the FA Youth Cup for the third time in four seasons – an incredible effort!

In a two-legged final against Manchester City, Joe Edwards' young side won 3-1 away and then secured the trophy with a 2-1 victory in the home game at Stamford Bridge. The team's captain, Charlie Colkett, was one of three players, along with Ola Aina and Jeremie Boga, to appear in his third Youth Cup final. As the competition is only open to players aged 16-18, it is not possible to appear in more than three finals, making their achievement all the more remarkable. Well done, lads!

As for the coach, Edwards was keen to point out how much of an inspiration the first team are to the young players in the Academy. After all, it's not every youth team that gets to watch the champions train at close quarters.

"Our boys take their lead from the first team because they set the example that if you want to be a Chelsea player then you have to be a winner," the Under-18s coach said.

"The way we're winning so consistently in this competition is a huge credit to everybody who works in the Academy. It's not just one team of players but a couple of cycles of players now and hopefully that winning mentality can continue in the coming years."

DREAM TEAM

Over the course of the 2014/15 season, the club's matchday programme interview
got the most votes together to form an ultimate Blues XI and the end product is a world-class side which w
ask an older relative about.

CENTRE-FORWARD
Didier Drogba

The man who sits in fourth place in our all-time scorers' list secured his place as a true Chelsea legend when he scored the equaliser and winning penalty in the 2012 Champions League final.

CENTRE-MIDFIELDER
Frank Lampard

The club's leading scorer of all time had a strike rate many centre-forwards would be proud of but, incredibly, he got all of his 211 goals from midfield. Lampard also netted 29 times in 106 appearances for England.

LEFT-WINGER
Eden Hazard

The Belgian international has made a huge impact since joining Chelsea in 2012, twice being named the club's Player of the Year as well as winning a host of other awards.

CENTRE-BACK
John Terry

Since making his debut in 1998, he has become the club's most successful captain of all time. Has won a remarkable 16 major trophies with the Blues and also became the highest-scoring defender in Premier League history in 2014/15.

LEFT-BACK
Ashley Cole

During his eight seasons with the Blues, Cole was not only regarded as one of the best full-backs in England, but the entire world. Capped 107 times at international level.

GOALKEEPER
Petr Cech

No goalkeeper in the club's history has won as much as Cech, who joined the Blues in 2004 and made 494 appearances before leaving in the summer. In fact, only two shot stoppers have played more Premier League games than Cech.

ferent well-known fan in each issue to find out their favourite Chelsea team of all time. We put the players who
ke some beating. Some of the players you will know from current or recent squads, and others you might have to

CENTRE-FORWARD
Peter Osgood

Nicknamed the King of Stamford Bridge, Peter Osgood is the only player who has been honoured with a statue at the stadium. A powerful, skilful striker who scored 150 goals in 380 appearances during the sixties and seventies.

CENTRE-MIDFIELDER
Dennis Wise

Before JT, Wise was our most successful captain of all time, having skippered us to two FA Cups, the League Cup and Cup Winners' Cup. Made 445 appearances, putting him seventh on our all-time list.

RIGHT-WINGER
Gianfranco Zola

Once voted by fans as the club's greatest-ever player, Zola joined the Blues in 1996 and scored 80 goals in 312 appearances. The skilful Italian always played with a smile on his face, and had a similar effect on supporters.

CENTRE-BACK
Marcel Desailly

The French centre-back joined the Blues as a World Cup winner in 1998. Nicknamed "The Rock", he was one of our regular defenders when John Terry was breaking into the team and helped our skipper become the player he is today.

RIGHT-BACK
Ron Harris

Commonly known as "Chopper", Ron Harris was a tough defender who has made more appearances for the club than anyone else, having played in an incredible 795 games from 1961 to 1980. It's a record that may never be broken!

SPOT THE DIFFERENCE

It would be daft not to meet a koala bear if you visited Australia and that's exactly what José Mourinho did in Sydney during our 2015 post-season tour. Can you spot seven differences between the two images?

Answers on p.61

WORD MAZE

Our Serbian right-back needs to get to the game, can you help him find his way to Stamford Bridge on time by spelling his full name on the grid?

```
    F   U   G   U   H   D
      B   R   A   H   N   G
B   V   N   V   N   Q   N   G
L   D   L   S   I   O   V   M
U   K   A   P   A   N   I   F
H   M   V   I   V   M   C   F
      L   R   Z   D   J   N
      Y   I   Q   Y   L   U
```

SQUAD NUMBER MATHS

It's time to do maths Chelsea style. Can you identify the players below and use their squad numbers in the sums to reveals the number of the missing player? Here's a tip, if you don't know the player's squad number, you can find them on **chelseafc.com**.

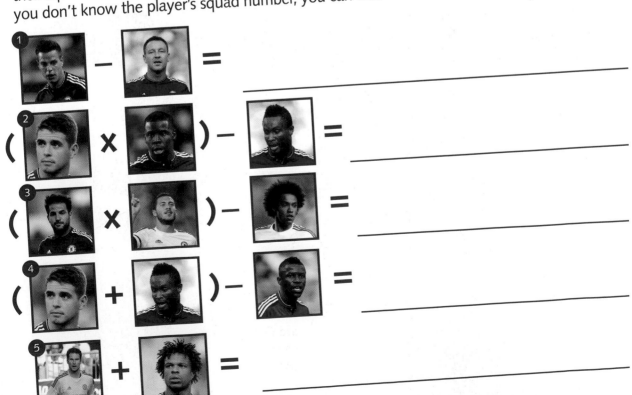

1. [ ] – [ ] = _____

2. ([ ] × [ ]) – [ ] = _____

3. ([ ] × [ ]) – [ ] = _____

4. ([ ] + [ ]) – [ ] = _____

5. [ ] + [ ] = _____

MEET THE CHELSEA LADIES

Chelsea Ladies made history in August 2015 when they lifted the FA Women's Cup in the first final ever to be held at Wembley Stadium – and, what's more, it was the first piece of silverware won by the Blues! We bring you the lowdown on Emma Hayes' side…

FA WOMEN'S CUP WINNERS 2015

A goal from Ji So-Yun was enough to see off Notts County Ladies in the FA Women's Cup final. Eni Aluko was selected as Player of the Match after a dazzling display on the wing, but it was a superb team effort. The Lady Magpies barely even had a shot on goal!

THE PLAYERS

JI SO-YUN
The South Korean star has been compared to Lionel Messi – and she proved what a superstar she is by scoring the winning goal at Wembley!

GEMMA DAVISON
Wing wizard Gemma Davison says she tries to play like Eden Hazard. When you see her fancy footwork and incredible pace, it's easy to see why she's been such a big signing for the Ladies!

ENIOLA ALUKO, KATIE CHAPMAN AND CLAIRE RAFFERTY
Chelsea provided three players to the England squad which finished third at the Women's World Cup in Canada, which was our best-ever performance at the tournament!

MARIJA BANUSIC AND HEDVIG LINDAHL
Goalkeeper Hedvig Lindahl conceded only once on her way to lifting the FA Women's Cup with the Blues! And her fellow Swede Marija Banusic is nicknamed Maredinho because her dad reckons she plays like Ronaldinho!

Chelsea Ladies play their home games at Wheatsheaf Park, which is in Staines-upon-Thames. **Tickets cost £3 for kids and £5 for adults**, although if you have a Chelsea FC season-ticket you can gain free entry (excluding Champions League game). You can find more information on **chelseafc.com**

WHEN WE WERE YOUNG

You probably know everything about your favourite Chelsea players now. Which position they play, who their best mates are, how they style their hair...but what about when they were young? We found out what the Blues stars were like as youngsters...

DEDICATION'S WHAT YOU NEED:

Our players had to work hard on their game to reach the top.

Cesc Fàbregas: I've always been a big football fanatic. On a Saturday, I used to play for two different teams – for the school and for the town. So, I used to play 7 v 7 in the morning and 11 v 11 in the afternoon.

Diego Costa: In Brazil, if you have a son, the first thing you give him is a football. That's the first gift, so my dad was no different. I grew up playing football on the streets with my friends and that's the school I had – the street football.

Oscar: Since I was a little boy everybody in Americana thought I would become a professional footballer. I started, as most Brazilians do, by playing on the street – from the age of five or six, we would play almost all the time on the street after school.

CHANGING PLACES:

Not every Chelsea player started out in their current position

Nemanja Matic: I was the number 10 – the maestro. My brother plays there now and he learned off me then – and he still does now!

Cesar Azpilicueta: I was always a striker when I was younger. Sometimes I played on the right wing or at right-back but I was a striker until the age of around 15 or 16.

I COULD HAVE BEEN A CONTENDER:

Some sportsmen can turn their hands to any game.

John Terry: I loved playing snooker – my uncle used to take me and my dad every Sunday and I was quite good at the time. I was entering competitions against men and got really into it for a couple of years. At a young age I was knocking in some decent breaks.

Thibaut Courtois: I was raised in a volleyball family – both my parents played – and that's a sport where also tall players have to dive quickly, so I think it helped me as a goalkeeper.

TEENAGE SOUND SYSTEM:

The music we love when we're young always stays with us

Willian: Pagode, a Brazilian type of music which is still my favourite now. I listened to a Brazilian band called Exaltasamba a lot.

Eden Hazard: Definitely French rap. Booba was my favourite.

Kurt Zouma: Akon – Right Now. I love this music, I listened to this with my friends in my room and I liked dancing – Logobi - an African dance. When I was with my friends we listened and danced every day.

FASHION POLICE: *What was cool when the Blues were in school?*

Branislav Ivanovic: I always remember when I was growing up at that time in Serbia, everybody tucked whatever they were wearing on top – shirts or jumpers - into their jeans with a big belt. These pictures look funny now!

Gary Cahill: I had a Burberry hat, the one with all the checks. I also had a really harsh skinhead, I did it myself, a DIY haircut.

Ramires: When I was young I had lots of different types of hairstyles. I had one where you grow the hair up on top, then you cut the sides and you use a comb to keep it up in a quiff.

Loic Remy: I had a lot of different haircuts growing up – I think I tried to find myself! I had dreadlocks, I had no hair sometimes and even now I'm trying to find a new look!

11-A-SIDE

Think you know your Chelsea stars? Below are the names of 11 Blues, but can you match the facts to the right player?

A I received a lot of awards in 2014/15, winning Chelsea Player of the Year, Chelsea Players' Player of the Year, Premier League Player of the Year, Football Writers' Association Player of the Year and Professional Footballers' Association Player of the Year.

B I have played international football for both Brazil, where I was born, and Spain, who I represented at the 2014 World Cup.

C I was the only Chelsea player to represent England in international football in 2015.

D I started at right-back in every single Premier League game of the 2014/15 season.

E I joined the Blues in 2011 but spent three seasons on loan at Atletico Madrid before returning to play in goal at Stamford Bridge for 2014/15.

F I won Chelsea's Goal of the Season award for the second year in a row in 2011/12, for my lob against Barcelona in the Champions League semi-final.

G I was one of two players who signed for Chelsea from Russian side Anzhi Makhachkala before the 2013/14 season, having played there and in Ukraine since leaving my native Brazil.

H I signed for Chelsea as a right-back from Marseille in 2012, but I have become a left-back under José Mourinho.

I I won my 11th cup final with Chelsea when we beat Tottenham at Wembley in 2015, but it was the first time I had scored in a final.

J I scored the first goal of my second spell at Chelsea in a 6-3 win over Everton in August 2014.

K I made my professional debut for a London club and have won the World Cup, two European Championships and the Spanish league title, but lifted the Premier League trophy for the first time in 2015.

☐ 2 Branislav Ivanovic	☐ 4 Cesc Fàbregas	☐ 7 Ramires
☐ 10 Eden Hazard	☐ 13 Thibaut Courtoi	☐ 18 Diego Costa
☐ 21 Nemanja Matic	☐ 22 Willian	☐ 24 Gary Cahill
☐ 26 John Terry	☐ 28 Cesar Azpilicueta	

WIN A SIGNED CHELSEA SHIRT!

Answer the following question correctly and you could win a Chelsea shirt signed by a first-team player.

The last time the colour red featured on the Chelsea home shirt was in 2010/11. Which player finished that season as our top scorer in all competitions?
A) Nicolas Anelka
B) Salomon Kalou
C) Daniel Sturridge

Entry is by e-mail only. Only one entry per contestant. Please enter CFC SHIRT followed by either A, B or C in the subject line of an email. In the body of the email, please include your full name, address, postcode, email address, phone number and date of birth and send to: frontdesk@grangecommunications.co.uk by Friday 25th March 2016.

Competition Terms and Conditions

1) The closing date for this competition is Friday 25th March 2016 at midnight. Entries received after that time will not be counted.

2) Information on how to enter and on the prize form part of these conditions.

3) Entry is open to those residing in the UK only. If entrants are under 18, consent from a parent or guardian must be obtained and the parent or guardian must agree to these terms and conditions. If entrants are under 13, this consent must be given in writing from the parent or guardian with their full contact details.

4) This competition is not open to employees or their relatives of Chelsea Football Club. Any such entries will be invalid.

5) The start date for entries is 30th October 2015 at 4pm.

6) Entries must be strictly in accordance with these terms and conditions. Any entry not in strict accordance with these terms and conditions will be deemed to be invalid and no prize will be awarded in respect of such entry. By entering, all entrants will be deemed to accept these rules.

7) One (1) lucky winner will win a 2015/16 season signed football shirt.

8) The prize is non-transferable and no cash alternative will be offered. Entry is by email only. Only one entry per contestant. Please enter CFC SHIRT followed by either A, B or C in the subject line of an email. In the body of the email, please include your full name, address, postcode, email address and phone number and send to: frontdesk@grangecommunications.co.uk by Friday 25th March 2016.

9) The winner will be picked at random. The winner will be contacted within 72 hours of the closing date. Details of the winner can be requested after this time from the address below.

10) Entries must not be sent in through agents or third parties. No responsibility can be accepted for lost, delayed, incomplete, or for electronic entries or winning notifications that are not received or delivered. Any such entries will be deemed void.

11) The winner will have 72 hours to claim their prize once initial contact has been made by the Promoter. Failure to respond may result in forfeiture of the prize.

12) At Chelsea FC plc and our group companies, we go the extra mile to ensure that your personal information is kept secure and safe. We will not release it to outside companies to use but we'd like your permission to keep in touch and tell you about relevant news, offers and promotions from ourselves and on behalf of our official sponsors and partners. If you would prefer not to receive these messages you can opt out by emailing CFC STOP to frontdesk@grangecommunications.co.uk before midnight on Friday 25th March 2016. Your information will always be safeguarded under the terms and conditions of the Data Protection Act 1998 and CFC's Privacy Policy (http://www.chelseafc.com/the-club/legal/privacy-policy.html) to ensure that the information you provide is safe.

13) The Promoter reserves the right to withdraw or amend the promotion as necessary due to circumstances outside its reasonable control. The Promoter's decision on all matters is final and no correspondence will be entered into.

14) The Promoter (or any third party nominated by the Promoter) may use the winner's name and image and their comments relating to the prize for future promotional, marketing and publicity purposes in any media worldwide without notice and without any fee being paid.

15) Chelsea Football Club's decision is final; no correspondence will be entered in to. Except in respect of death or personal injury resulting from any negligence of the Club, neither Chelsea Football Club nor any of its officers, employees or agents shall be responsible for (whether in tort, contract or otherwise):
 (i) any loss, damage or injury to you and/or any guest or to any property belonging to you or any guest in connection with this competition and/or the prize, resulting from any cause whatsoever;
 (ii) for any loss of profit, loss of use, loss of opportunity or any indirect, economic or consequential losses whatsoever.

16) This competition shall be governed by English law.

17) Promoter: Grange Communications Ltd, 22 Great King Street, Edinburgh EH3 6QH.

PAST LIFE

Can you name which of our current players signed for the Blues from these clubs?

1. Bolton Wanderers.
2. Marseille.
3. KRC Genk.
4. Lokomotiv Moscow.
5. Barcelona.
6. Benfica.

GIMME FIVE

Diego Costa was one of Chelsea's biggest success stories last season. Can you answer these five questions on the hotshot?

1. Diego Costa joined us from which Spanish club?
2. Who did he score his first competitive Chelsea goal against?
3. In the fourth game of last season, he netted a hat-trick. Who was that against?
4. Who does Diego play international football for?
5. What brand of boots does he wear?

Now it's time for five tricky teasers on our captain, leader, legend John Terry

TRUE OR FALSE?

1. JT has played for Nottingham Forest.
2. He has made more appearances than any other Chelsea player.
3. He is the highest-scoring defender in Premier League history.
4. He has won more trophies than any other Blues captain.
5. He made his first-team debut in 2004.

Answers on p.61

CHELSEA FC:
THROUGH THE DECADES

Chelsea turned 110 years old during the 2014/15 season and the club has come a long way since it was formed way back in 1905. Here we look at some of the biggest events in the club's history…

Although it seems hard to imagine nowadays, Chelsea have spent time outside the Premier League, or Division One as it used to be known. We began life in Division Two for the 1905/06 season - our first promotion to the top flight came in 1907.

1900s

World War One had a big impact on football, with the leagues as we knew them stopping for three years as many players were called up to fight for their country. Just before the cancellation of the national divisions, Chelsea reached our first FA Cup final in 1915, but lost 3-0 to Sheffield United.

1910s

Nowadays, players have their name and number on the back of their shirts, but that wasn't always the case. In fact, players' shirts didn't even have numbers on until 1928, when Chelsea became the first team in England to introduce them.

1920s

With all fans having a seat at Stamford Bridge these days, the capacity of the stadium is considerably smaller than it used to be. Our record crowd is 82,905, which came against Arsenal in October 1935. The game ended in a 1-1 draw.

1930s

World War Two dominated the first half of this decade and Stamford Bridge was bombed in October 1940. Luckily, damage to the stadium was minimal.

1955 Roy Bentley

Chelsea were crowned champions of England for the first time when we won the old First Division in 1955. Back then, the team was managed by Ted Drake and captained by club legend Roy Bentley. We sealed the triumph with a 3-0 win over Sheffield Wednesday at Stamford Bridge.

Manager Ted Drake congratulates his skipper

Chelsea reached their second cup final fifty years after their first, and this time there was a happier ending. We beat Leicester City 3-2 over two legs to win the 1965 League Cup.

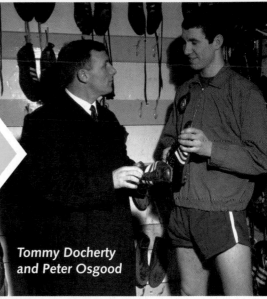

Tommy Docherty and Peter Osgood

A key spell in Chelsea's history saw us record two historic moments. In 1970, we lifted our first FA Cup, beating bitter rivals Leeds United in a replay at Old Trafford. The following year, we captured our first European honour, when we beat Real Madrid in Athens, again in a replay, to lift the Cup Winners' Cup.

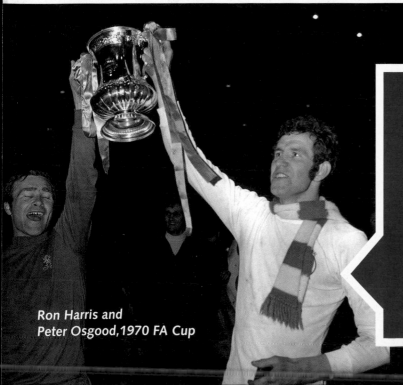

Ron Harris and Peter Osgood, 1970 FA Cup

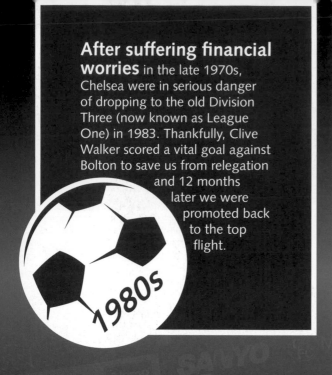

After suffering financial worries in the late 1970s, Chelsea were in serious danger of dropping to the old Division Three (now known as League One) in 1983. Thankfully, Clive Walker scored a vital goal against Bolton to save us from relegation and 12 months later we were promoted back to the top flight.

1980s

Roberto Di Matteo opens the scoring after just 43 seconds

The Premier League began in 1992, but Chelsea's success in this decade came in the cup competitions. After signing lots of world-class stars, we won the FA Cup in 1997 and the following season claimed the League Cup and Cup Winners' Cup. The good times were returning to Stamford Bridge.

1990s

(Premier League champions for first time, 2005)

After Roman Abramovich bought the club in 2003, our fortunes transformed beyond belief. José Mourinho arrived as manager a year later and secured back-to-back Premier League titles in 2005 and 2006. There was also considerable success in the domestic cup competitions, although success in the Champions League continued to evade us, despite reaching the final for the first time in 2008, when we lost on penalties to Manchester United in Moscow.

2000s

Our first domestic Double

(winning the Premier League and FA Cup in the same season) came in 2010 and two years later we won the Champions League for the first time, beating Bayern Munich in their own stadium on penalties in a dramatic final. Europa League success in 2013 made us the only British team to have won every UEFA club honour. José Mourinho's return brought us Premier League and League Cup triumphs in 2015 and the future looks very bright indeed for the Blues.

Victory parade after winning the Double

DOUBLE WINNERS
09 — 10

2010s

José returns

Didier Drogba who scored the winning penalty in the shootout of the 2012 Champions League final

DID YOU KNOW?

Chelsea Football Club was formed in a pub opposite Stamford Bridge which still stands to this day. Back then it was known as the Rising Sun. Now it's called the Butcher's Hook.

The club marked its 110th birthday in many ways. One of them was to produce a special matchday programme in the same style as the ones created over a century ago; this time with Eden Hazard pictured on the front.

Our first goalkeeper was called Willie Foulke, but he was commonly known by the nickname "Fatty" due to the fact he stood 6ft 4ins tall and weighed well over 20 stone.

p.27 WORD SEARCH

p.45 SPOT THE DIFFERENCE:

p.47 WORD MAZE

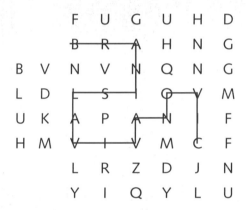

p.47 SQUAD NUMBER MATHS

1. Azpilicueta (28) – Terry (26) = Ivanovic (2)
2. Oscar (8) x Zouma (5) – Mikel (12) = Azpilicueta (28)
3. Fàbregas (4) x Hazard (10) – Willian (22) = Remy (18)
4. Oscar (8) + Mikel (12) – Ramires (7) = Courtois (13)
5. Begovic (1) + Remy (18) = Costa (19)

p.52 11-A-SIDE:

Ivanovic – D

Fàbregas – K

Ramires – F

Hazard – A

Courtois – E

Costa – B

Matic – J

Willian – G

Cahill – C

Terry – I

Azpilicueta – H

p.55 PAST LIFE

1. Gary Cahill.
2. Cesar Azpilicueta.
3. Thibaut Courtois.
4. Branislav Ivanovic.
5. Cesc Fàbregas.
6. Ramires.

p.55 GIMME FIVE

1. Atletico Madrid.
2. Burnley.
3. Swansea City.
4. Spain.
5. Adidas.

p.55 JOHN TERRY TRUE OR FALSE?

1. True – he was on loan there in the 1998/99 season.
2. False – he's third on the list.
3. True – 39 Premier League goals.
4. True.
5. False – it was way back in October 1998.

WHERE'S STAMFORD?